SUPER COMMUNICATION

Forthcoming titles in this series will include

- *Winning CVs*
- *Win–Win Negotiation*
- *Coping with Company Politics*
- *How to Wow an Audience*
- *How to Pay Less Tax*
- *Make the Most of Meetings*
- *Key Account Management*

Do you have ideas for subjects which could be included in this exciting and innovative series? Could your company benefit from close involvement with a forthcoming title?

Please contact David Grant Publishing Limited
80 Ridgeway, Pembury, Tunbridge Wells, Kent TN2 4EZ
Tel/fax +44 (0)1892 822886
Email GRANTPUB@aol.com
with your ideas or suggestions.

SUPER COMMUNICATION

THE NLP WAY

Russell Webster

60 Minutes Success Skills Series

Copyright © David Grant Publishing Limited 2000

First published 2000 by
David Grant Publishing Limited
80 Ridgeway
Pembury
Kent TN2 4EZ
United Kingdom

01   00   10 9 8 7 6 5 4 3 2 1

60 Minutes Success Skills Series is an imprint of
David Grant Publishing Limited

All rights reserved. Except for the quotation of short passages for the purposes of criticism and review, no part of this publication may be reproduced, stored in a retrieval system, or transmitted, in any form or by any means, electronic, mechanical, photocopying, recording or otherwise, without the prior permission of the publisher.

British Library Cataloguing in Publication Data
A CIP catalogue record for this book is available from the British Library

ISBN 1-901306-22-4

Cover design: Liz Rowe
Text design: Graham Rich
Production editor: Paul Stringer
Copy-editor: Kim Latham

Typeset in Futura by
Archetype IT Ltd, web site http://www.archetype-it.com
Printed and bound in Great Britain by
T.J. International Ltd, Padstow, Cornwall

This book is printed on acid-free paper

The publishers accept no responsibility for any investment or financial decisions made on the basis of the information in this book. Readers are advised always to consult a qualified financial adviser.

All names mentioned in the text have been changed to protect the identity of the business people involved. Any resemblance to existing companies or people is entirely coincidental.

Contents

Welcome! About *Super Communication the NLP Way*   7

Chapter 1: Don't we all do it anyway?   9
Learning to listen
Targeting your audience
Importance of body language
How to be a great communicator

Chapter 2: Linking people together   19
Dispute resolution
Mind reading
Building rapport
Discovering what makes people tick

Chapter 3: People are different   31
Distinguishing between matchers and mismatchers
Rules for confident communication
Dealing with difficult people

Chapter 4: FROGS and AARDVARCs   41
Learning to accept people
Understanding people's needs
Asking open questions
How to listen effectively
Using other people's interests to your advantage

Chapter 5: Specifically speaking   53
Precision model
Five powerful words
Word power
Having the right answers to difficult questions
Self-confidence – talk it like you walk it
People hear your music, not your words

Welcome!

ABOUT *SUPER COMMUNICATION WITH NLP*

Can you really learn enough in just one hour to help you to be a better communicator? The answer is a resounding "Yes" although, as with all things, it will take practice to master. This book provides you with a blueprint which will point you in all of the right directions, and gives you lots of tips and techniques that will show you how to be a super communicator.

Is this book for you?

Do you frequently find yourself in the situation, either at work or in your private life, when you have come away from a conversation and known that you haven't got your message across properly? You might even have caused upset despite having no intention to do so. If you feel that you could benefit from learning how to make yourself fully understood, then this is the book for you!

As you start to combine the insights and the information contained in *Super Communication*, you should find that communicating and interacting with others will come more naturally to you. As that happens you will find your self-confidence growing. Since confidence, along with sincerity, is a vital factor in effective communications, this in turn will enhance your skills, resulting in a further increase in confidence. It's a dynamic upward spiral which you can continue as far as you want to take it.

As with most subjects it's not necessary to understand every last thing before you begin to use the material. If you feel that there are any areas of your life where you could benefit from being a better communicator then you will be able to take some of the lessons of this book, put them into practice and enjoy the rewards of more confident communication while you carry on learning. One small piece of knowledge can make a significant difference to your whole life. Focusing on just one aspect of this book – listening attentively, for example – will bring massive benefits to your business life, social life and your most important relationships.

About the author

Building on many years' experience as a sales trainer and consultant, Russell Webster formed Mindworld Publishing, an innovative company in the field of audio books on human nature, personal development and training. He is highly regarded as an eloquent and gifted speaker and narrator and already has several best-selling audio books to his name.

About the 60 Minutes Series

The 60 Minutes Success Skills Series is written for people with neither the time nor the patience to trawl through acres of jargon, management-speak and page-filling waffle. Like all the books in the series, *Super Communication* has been written in the belief that you can learn all you really need to know quickly and without hassle. The aim is to distil the essential, practical advice you can use straight away.

The principles expounded in *Super Communication* are a mixture of research, common sense and proven fact. They also call on pure psychology, and on advanced, applied psychologies such as Eriksonian linguistics and neuro-linguistic programming, both of which are considered to be at the cutting edge of understanding how human beings communicate.

But isn't communication just a fancy word for talking – and don't we all do it anyway? Read on and you'll find out the reality!

DON'T WE ALL DO IT ANYWAY?

Chapter

What's in this chapter for you

Learning to listen
Targeting your audience
Importance of body language
How to be a great communicator

The vital skill

> How many presentations have you sat through in your career? How many training courses? What can you remember of all those lessons you learned at school or college? In fact, if you stop to think about it, how much of what you are supposed to have learned has stayed with you and is relevant to what you actually do today?

During your school years you probably learned quite a lot about maths, English, art, geography, physics, biology and chemistry. You may even have passed some fairly advanced examinations on these subjects. But how much of that do you remember, need to remember, or use on a day-to-day basis? Probably little or none.

> *❝ I've been on lots of training courses over the years, and I can honestly say that most of them went in one ear and out the other. The information was good but, more often than not, it was presented in such a tedious way that I forgot it almost immediately. The courses that worked for me were given by people that realise it's not just the message that's important, but the way it's put across. That's successful communication. ❞*
> **– Jill Parks, customer services manager**

Do you remember the interesting people who taught you? We've all got memories of eccentric teachers, passionate about their subjects, who brought their subjects alive; the silly examples they used and odd bits of information they presented that stick in the memory.

> ❝ *When I left school I couldn't speak in front of a crowd of people, and I was really in awe of the older people. It seems absolutely ludicrous that, after all the theory, facts and figures, the one thing they didn't try to teach you was how to communicate with those around you.* ❞
> **– Ray McLeod, sales executive**

The one thing that you will have had to do more than anything else in adult life is to deal with people. When you work for or with them, or have them work for you, you have to try to understand and motivate them – you need to interact with them, console them, support them, like them, love them, and generally build a relationship with them.

Dealing with people can be difficult, even people we think we are close to. Marriages break up, friends and families have bust-ups that seem irretrievable, children and parents don't talk to one another, business relationships founder, career problems arise, battles rage in the workplace, neighbours go to war, and so too do nations.

Ninety-nine times out of a hundred it is a lack of communication, an inability to communicate, or a communication breakdown that causes the problems. Surely that makes communication one of the most important things that you will ever have to learn.

> Being able to communicate effectively is vital in every walk of life. If you didn't learn how to at school, then you should start now.

> ❝ *It seems amazing to me how many of the people I have worked for were dreadful bosses, because they seemed incapable of communicating properly. They treated their staff like automata, and never took time out to try to find out what motivated people, what made them happy, what they liked about their jobs. I don't think it was arrogance on their part, simply an inability, maybe even a fear, of getting close.* ❞
> **– June Fraser, civil servant**

For many people, their overriding regret in life is that they spent a vast proportion of their time wrapped up in the quest for material wealth and success, and failed to take enough time out to communicate to their loved ones – their families, their partners, their children and their close friends – how they felt about them. Some of them had simply not known how, some had not taken the time, and others had always put it off until later.

> Do you take time out to express to others what you feel about them? Are you comfortable telling people at work that they have done a good job? Can you say "thank you" and not feel compromised? Would life be better at work and at home if you could communicate your feelings better to those around you?

This book is all about communication. It is about how to communicate effectively and how to get people to communicate with you. It is about why good communication is necessary if you are to have excellent relationships with people both in business and in your social life.

The listening skill

Of course this book is a form of communication, using printed words to convey information. That can be a very effective way of getting a message across, but it won't reach everyone. What about people who don't read books? Some of them might prefer an audio version and some might rather watch a video. Even then, books, audios and videos are all one-way communications. This has important parallels when dealing with people face-to-face.

Good listening skills are crucial to effective communication.

> " *My ex-husband thought a good conversation meant him talking at me, and not responding in any way to anything I said. It drove me mad – he'd just never listen to me!* "
> **– Pam Oliver, divorcee**

Most of us are not very good at listening. When we should be listening we're busy thinking about what we want to say next. We're so eager to impress with the next clever thing we're going to come out with that we don't have time to take in what is being said to us. But it has been suggested that the real reason we don't listen carefully to one another is fear. Fear?

> Are you afraid of change? If you really listen to what someone says, then you might truly understand them and may be forced to change the way you see things. That sort of deep-rooted change can be very disturbing. What we do instead is to reinterpret the other person's point so that it fits with our existing views, or just reject it altogether – so there is no real communication. And if that is what you and I do to other people when they are trying to communicate with us, then what do you imagine they do when it is our turn?

> *I don't understand my son, he doesn't listen to a word I say!*
> **– Miriam Harris, exasperated mother**

Think about this quote; re-read it slowly: "I don't understand my son, he doesn't listen to a word I say!" How can you understand someone if you are doing the talking? And how can you possibly communicate with someone if you don't understand them?

The audience

The first rule of communication is to match your message to the audience. You have to try to assimilate yourself into the environment you are addressing, take on board what signals you can pick up, and work on this. The following quote is a perfect example of where so many people go wrong.

> *We had a whizz-kid new boss who was brought in to 'revolutionise' the way we work. He was full of mission statements and management gobbledegook, which may have gone down well in his last job in the City, but meant nothing to us. We were having to deal with people in dreadful housing, with awful social problems, and this stuff just came from another planet. Once he realised that, and matched his message to our circumstances, he actually had some brilliant ideas.*
> **– Ray Fleming, housing officer**

> Always make sure you know who you are talking to. Find out about the other person before you start trying to make yourself understood, and match your message to your audience.

If another person's values are completely different to yours, nothing you say is likely to register with them, unless you take the trouble to find out what makes them tick first.

> What motivates you? Can you think of anyone whose motivators are different to yours? How might you communicate most effectively with them?

More than words can say

Communication is not just about the words we use. In fact, research shows that we communicate more with our gestures and expressions, our body language, than we do with the words we use. So this book is about the different types of communication we can use, not just the words, and it is also about learning how to listen.

> Start to notice your body language, and other people's. See how much you can pick up about what someone is saying just by watching them.

What makes a great communicator?

> " *History was my most loathed subject at school until I had this great new teacher. She'd come into the classroom like a whirlwind, full of enthusiasm for that day's lesson, and transform dull dates and facts into fascinating stories. She captivated all of us.* "
> **– Jeffrey Dartwood, historian**

What is it about some people that makes them able to get their point across quickly and easily? How do people hold large audiences spellbound and send them away wanting more? Is it their ability to tell stories or amuse people? Is it their ability to put their point across succinctly and elegantly? Is it their ability to command people's full attention? Or perhaps it's to do with their non-verbal communication: the way they use their eyes, and other elements of their body language?

Well, yes, to some extent it has to do with all of these things and a little more besides – a certain *je ne sais quoi*, a certain air and a certain confidence. But that poses the question: can anyone become a good communicator? And I believe the answer to this question is that everyone can learn how to communicate more effectively and confidently, just as you now take for granted things that you learned to do as a child, such as riding a bicycle.

The chances are that the first time you tried to ride a bicycle you fell off, and also the second time, and the third time, and possibly a few more times after that. At that stage you experienced what is known as *conscious incompetence*. You were suddenly, and perhaps painfully, made aware of the fact that you were not too good at bicycle riding.

However, with perseverance, most people do eventually learn to ride a bike without falling off. If you reached the stage at which you could stay upright and pedal along on your own then you developed what is known as *conscious competence*. In this stage you know that you can ride a bicycle, but you still have to concentrate on what you're doing in order to succeed.

Eventually, however, if you carried on, you almost certainly stopped thinking about it and just jumped on your bike and rode off whenever the fancy took you; it just came naturally to you, and you could think about other things whilst you were riding. You'd reached a level called *unconscious competence*, where being good at it took no real conscious thought.

> If your communication as a child and teenager, perhaps even as an adult, was not successful then it's more than likely that you grew up believing that you weren't very good at communicating, and maybe still believe this. This puts you into conscious incompetence, and can be very damaging from a self-confidence point of view.

DON'T WE ALL DO IT ANYWAY?

Some people reach a plateau at a level somewhere between conscious incompetence and conscious competence. Sometimes things work really well for them, they get the results they want and everything is great. Then at other times it all goes wrong, and they can never quite work out why.

Even more frustratingly, if you're stuck at this stage, you know there's something wrong (that's the conscious incompetence working), but you don't know what it is.

> *When I was a child, I watched my big brother riding his bike. It looked as simple as walking. So, when my brother wasn't looking I grabbed his bike and jumped up on to the saddle. Next thing I knew, my head made contact with the path. I've still got the scar and a healthy streak of respect for new challenges I have to tackle.*
> **– George Spencer, building contractor**

There is in fact an earlier stage. Before you started to learn to ride a bike you were on the starting blocks of competence, at a level called *unconscious incompetence*. In other words, cycling looked easy enough but you were no good at it, and you didn't realise it! How could you?

In terms of communication there are those who are still at that level. They are not very good and they don't know it. These poor communicators seem to turn up everywhere, usually looking for new targets to bore to the point where strangulation seems to be the kindest option. Some of them even invite themselves to come and sit with you just when you're having an in-depth conversation with someone else, because that way they'll have a ready-made audience.

> Whereabouts on the communication scale are you? Do you have minimum self-confidence at all times, or do you find that sometimes you work extremely well, really get your message through, while at others you simply flounder? Can you identify symptoms about yourself which tie in with how you react?

The winning edge in business – and in life

The first thing to be clear about, though, is that confidence has to be learned. From the moment you left school until the day that you die, your ability to communicate effectively has influenced, and will influence, your career, your finances, your love life, your relationships with your children, your friendships, ... everything. So pause for a moment and consider: has your communication ever let you down?

When did you last get into an argument, or leave yourself or someone else upset at the end of a conversation? Or perhaps you can think of a time when you just failed to get your point across – when someone simply did not understand you.

> *I had what I thought was the most amazing invention. I showed it to my friends and they all agreed – it was brilliant! But I couldn't communicate it to the people that mattered. I went to the bank, and to various venture capital companies, but I couldn't convince them. I wanted to enthuse them with the product spec. and my marketing strategy, while they were just interested in the bottom-line issues. I just couldn't reach them!*
> **– Jim Pearce, inventor**

It's the same right through life. You may have a passionate desire to further the cause of a particular charity, or help an organisation close to your heart, but if you cannot get that passion across to other people how will you enlist their support? There are so many other occasions when you simply must be able to communicate effectively. You may need to borrow money from your bank manager. You may want to nurture a new business client or resolve a dispute in the office. You might want to make a date with a friend or just tell someone about your day. Actually, from the moment you wake up in the morning to the moment you go to sleep at night you will spend the majority of the day communicating with someone, even if it is only yourself.

If you need convincing further about the most vital skill of all, then look at what happens when communications break down, or simply do not exist.

> *To jaw-jaw is always better than to war-war.*
> **– Winston Churchill**

DON'T WE ALL DO IT ANYWAY?

The ultimate breakdown in communication is war, whether war between nations, between neighbours, or between husbands and wives.

So why do communications break down? We'll find out in Chapter 2.

> There is more to communicating than you might think:
>
> 1. Communication is not just about talking – it's about listening too.
> 2. We communicate more with our body language than we do with our words. Learn to be aware of your own and other's body language.
> 3. Be honest with people. Good communication is about sincere understanding – it is not a question of clever techniques and tricks.
> 4. Be honest with yourself – do you try to do all the talking in conversations, or do you sit quietly and let others talk rather than making the points you wanted to?

LINKING PEOPLE TOGETHER
— Chapter ❷

What's in this chapter for you

> *Dispute resolution*
> *Mind reading*
> *Building rapport*
> *Discovering what makes people tick*

Non-verbal communication

Of all of the things that separate you and I from the animal kingdom, perhaps the most telling is speech – the ability to communicate with words. Indeed, most people think of effective communication as being a purely verbal thing. But does the bookie at the racecourse use words to signal over to other bookies? What about the stock market trader? There may be plenty of frantic shouting going on, but it is the hand signals that perform most of the transactions. And then what about the person who made a particular gesture to you with his finger in the rush hour traffic? Did you know what he meant, and did you perhaps make a gesture in reply? So do we need words to communicate, or are they in fact a bonus?

> Have you ever left a business meeting and felt you just didn't get your point across? Or had a deal go amazingly well? What was going on – was it in the words you used or something else?

Well, amazingly, in external communication words are the least important of all. Consider this for a moment: if a member of the opposite sex came up to you, wrapped their arms around you, looked deeply and lovingly into your eyes and said fondly, "I really don't like you very much," what message might you be getting? How important are the actual words?

> Notice people's body language. Assess what messages you might be sending.

The fact is that only seven per cent of your communication is through the words that you use. A much larger percentage, thirty-eight per cent to be precise, is through the intonation and voice inflection that you use, and by far the most important part of your communication, fifty-five per cent, is through your body language or non-verbal communication. From your facial expression to your body posture, from your breathing patterns to your arm, hand and eye movements, every part of you sends out a message.

> *I'd been out celebrating a major business deal but forgot to tell my wife that I'd be home late. I opened the front door and found her glowering at me, her arms folded, her lips compressed, steam coming out of her ears. She didn't have to say anything for me to know what was going through her mind.*
> **– Peter Ellis, management consultant**

Another example is that little eye roll that says, "He's making such a fool of himself." One hundred per cent communication with one gesture!

When communication breaks down

As a youngster I was not a confident communicator. However, I consider that, over the years, I have learned to become a more than reasonable communicator. So it was rather ironic that I should find myself spending four days filming with Carlton TV for an episode of Neighbours from Hell, about a dispute that really boiled down to a lack of communication. What happened?

It started like this. I was allowing my neighbours, who happened to be the new owners of a nightclub I used to own, to use my land to store their large bottle bins, at no charge. It seemed the neighbourly thing to do; at least until I needed to develop the rest of the site and build the proposed lifeskills centre.

I'd already converted a disused building into what was destined to become the caretaker's house for the whole project, and temporarily moved in myself. Before long, however, the situation started to become unworkable. The new nightclub owners decided to empty the small bottle bins from their night's festivities into the large metal containers at three in the morning. Worse, when the metal bins were full they started to simply tip the empty bottles on the ground, creating an eyesore and a potential environmental health problem. And then, every two weeks a tipper lorry turned up and emptied the bins at five in the morning, waking everyone up!

I began by attempting to verbally communicate my displeasure at what I saw as the abuse of my goodwill. Then I tried writing. Two polite yet firm letters were followed by a legal letter, and all to no avail. The situation continued; in fact it deteriorated.

> Can you see how the breakdown of communication becomes an escalation of conflict? What could you do to save the situation?

The nightclub took to opening their doors at night and trying to blast me out with noise. I decided that the best answer to that was for me to fit a new sound system in my home – five thousand watts' worth to be precise. Then I just turned my system up a little louder than theirs. It was somewhere around this point that the issue hit the national press. What I'd done was create a confrontation, which was at least some form of communication. The only problem was that I've never been very keen on fisticuffs and had to decline an offer to communicate in that manner. The confrontation did however begin the process of communication, and I found a different way to solve the problem. I created some leverage and used a third party.

Remember Churchill and his "jaw-jaw" rather than "war-war"? What happened here was that the two sides stopped talking – and our non-verbal communications simply escalated the tensions and discontent on both sides.

> Analyse a breakdown of communication, either one you were involved in or one you know of. Did it start with little things and then escalate? If so, how could it have been stopped earlier?

There's a moral to this story: if all normal forms of communication break down then the only way forward may be to find and use a go-between: a mediator or arbitrator who's respected by both parties. On the world scale this "shuttle diplomacy" is often the only way to bring an end to conflict. It frequently takes a lot of "talks about talks" just to bring two opposing sides to the same table.

So if you ever have a problem that needs resolving, maybe a difficult dispute or a situation in which you have not spoken to someone for a long time, then the answer may be to find a go-between. But that is really just a preliminary to arriving at a situation where both parties can, and do, sit down opposite each other. It is only when you are actually sitting down with someone that you can engage all your senses and intuition and use all the various forms of communication to their best effect.

> Don't let disputes fester. If communication has broken down, use a third party to restart the process.

Reading people's minds

Some people believe that words will become all but superfluous in centuries to come and that we will all be able to read one another's minds. Some anthropologists in the past have reported instances of what they thought was telepathic communication between members of native tribes far from civilisation. Wherever the truth lies I do know that on many occasions someone has turned around to me and said, "How on earth could you have known what I was thinking?" I normally say that it's only intuition or "just a hunch". The truth is that I've actually practised, and become quite good at, reading people's body language and tone of voice. You too could learn how to do that.

It is no great secret that the body is controlled by the mind or, at any rate, the brain. From every heartbeat to every hormonal secretion, every step you take, every move you make, even every eye movement, part of you is monitoring and controlling what you do.

When you decide, in your mind, that it is time to relax, you sit down, sprawl out, and undergo a complete change of body posture and facial expression. Even your voice alters in character: often your speech becomes slower, deeper and more relaxed.

> Pretend that you're in a waiting room and act as if you're really bored. Notice how your posture changes. Your brain says, "I'm bored," and as if by magic your body responds: maybe you shuffle your feet or fold your arms. It's not just your body that changes; your facial expression alters too. You might assume a rather vacant expression and your eyes begin to wander, or perhaps you pull a slightly unusual face. Now if someone was watching you, would they say that you looked bored? Your non-verbal communication will have given the game away.

How do you stand when you're really annoyed? Try it and, as you do, notice how dramatically the change in your posture affects the way you feel. There is an important lesson in this about how we communicate inwardly, in other words how we communicate with ourselves. Our physiology, the way we stand or sit or move, is directly linked with our internal representations of the world – with how we feel. So if you want to feel excited, dynamic and vibrant, then act that way. Act as if you felt like that and very soon you will.

> Imagine that you are really, really excited about something. If life's a bit of a drag and there's nothing to get excited about, take a trip back in time and remember being very young and very excited about something: you might be just about to open a Christmas present, or perhaps it's the last day of term, or you're about to leave on a two-week holiday in the sunshine. Think yourself right back into what you felt like then. If you do this with enthusiasm, not only will you have the feeling of excitement, you will have the physiology of excitement too – your body posture and facial expression will be reflecting what you are feeling.

What's going on here? Well, as you change the thoughts going through your mind, your body changes to be in empathy with your mind. You could say that your body is a reflection of what's going on in your mind. To understand what's going through someone else's mind, reflect their body. In neuro-linguistic programming this is called *matching and mirroring*. If you learn the process of matching and mirroring you'll not only learn how to read people's minds; you'll also learn one of the secrets of creating instant rapport with other people.

Rapport is originally a French word meaning to be in connection with someone, but its more precise meaning is to be in harmony, or even in an emotional bond with someone.

> Have you ever noticed, or been lucky enough to experience, the incredible rapport that two people who are totally and utterly in love share with each other?

Imagine for a moment two people sitting at a table together, very obviously in love and deeply engrossed in one another. She has her chin resting in the palms of her hands and her elbows are on the table. She is breathing at a certain pace, talking at a certain pace, and looking in a certain way. He is sitting opposite her – and is a total mirror image of her. His chin is also resting in his palms, his elbows are resting on the table in just the same way. He is breathing and talking at the same pace and looking at her in the same manner. They are a total mirror image of one another, even down to the details of their facial expression.

> Envisage a different couple, in different circumstances, also in love. The details of their posture can be however you imagine them to be, but as long as you hold the idea of rapport they will match.

This is actually a major clue to creating rapport even with someone you've never met before. You can do it with somebody at the far end of a table, or someone standing twenty yards away.

> Observe someone's body posture, and then mould yours to match, or mirror, theirs. Watch their body movements and copy them. Don't be too obvious, or you may cause offence! But if they're gently stroking their chin then you do the same. If they have a little nervous habit such as moving an object around on

> the table then do the same. It doesn't have to be the same object, just so long as you make a similar action in the same manner.

I once had a most extraordinary experience with this. A colleague of mine was making a sales pitch to a third party, a stranger. Since my job was to sit quietly and not say anything, I began to match the posture and movements of the stranger. I had been doing this for some time with no result at all when I suddenly realised that his breathing pattern was completely different to mine. I was very relaxed, breathing deeply, using my diaphragm. He was breathing very rapidly and high up in his chest. The instant I began to breathe like that a thought flashed into my mind: "Can I trust this man?" The rational part of my mind instantly began to say things like, "Well, you hardly know him, but he seems all right." Then I suddenly realised that this was what he was thinking about my colleague. That is the power of matching and mirroring.

> Mirror people closely and accurately, especially their breathing, and start to make it a habit. This will begin to tell you what they are really thinking and feeling.

Another term for this is understudying, just like an actor or actress does in preparation for stepping into someone else's shoes. If you want to step into someone else's life, or wish them to step into yours, then mastering this process will help you to start creating that all-important rapport that must exist between two people in any successful social or business transaction.

When you're skilled at this a funny thing might happen to you, as it has to me and to others I know who are good at understudying, or matching and mirroring. The person that you've been understudying will come up to you and say, "Don't we know each other from somewhere?" They will be interested in you and your reply, because they feel as though they have some rapport with you. So they are already interested in what you have to say – what an opportunity!

> Start understudying and see if you can draw someone to you! That is the first step towards great communications.

The concept of reading someone's mind is not a space-age fantasy. It is simply the art of reading someone's body. Practise it with a friend or with your partner. Ask them to put their mind in a certain frame or state, without them telling you what it is. Ask them to allow their body to reflect that frame of mind while you try to work out what they are portraying. Do it without matching and mirroring, and then do it with. See which you find easier. Make the situations gradually more difficult until you absolutely have to match and mirror them, and find yourself in the same state of mind as they are; a little like losing your own identity and assuming theirs. The more you practise this the better you will become. Eventually you will find that you can develop the skill of reading people's minds.

Problems with wavelengths

If you've found yourself desperate to escape from someone's far from scintillating company, the chances are that you simply were not in tune with them, not on the same wavelength.

> Have you ever escaped from a conversation and thought to yourself, "Mmm, don't mind if I don't" – don't meet them again, that is, or don't have to communicate with them again – and responded to their cheery "See you soon!" with a forced smile and the thought, "Not if I see you first"?

There is of course just a small chance that either you or they were in fact totally uninteresting, but we shall ignore this possibility because everyone is interesting when you learn how to communicate more effectively.

> Before you dismiss somebody as completely uninteresting ask yourself how much you did to find out about them before making that judgement. Good communicators do not write people off.

We know that communication is contained in our words, our intonation and our body language yet different people place more importance on one of the three types than others. Suppose I walked up to someone and said, "Mary, we've had some wonderful times together recently and I've really come to know you very well these last few months. I have to say that I think I'm starting to like you so much that I want to spend the rest of my life with you." Now Mary might swoon at my feet and declare undying love for me, which would be a successful communication. But what if she said, "Talk's cheap! If you mean it then show me that you love me!"?

So, alternatively, I could walk up to Mary, reach out with both hands, look at her lovingly, pull her gently towards me, and wrap her tightly with a warm, caring hug. Do I need words to express my feelings? For Mary this type of communication might be much more meaningful.

> Think of a time when you used a wrong form of communication, or when someone used one on you. What was it that really went wrong, and what could you do about it?

Mind methods – what makes people tick?

To be a really great communicator you need to learn about what makes people tick, and how people tick differently from one another. Although all human beings share many traits and needs that are common to everyone, we do not all do things the same way. People process information in different ways – and to do it they have what are known as *mind methods*. Each one of us has a different method of communicating with ourselves and others, a different mind method.

Everyone has a mind method, but we don't all use the same one all the time. There are three predominant mind methods with which people process information, interpret their experiences and relate to others. To communicate successfully with others it's important to match their mind method. You will fairly quickly recognise which of the three is most like you.

The first type of mind method is the *visual* person. He or she will tend to speak quite quickly and will talk about "*seeing* the big *picture*", "gaining an *insight*" or "having a *vision*". They tend to interpret the world in visual form and are sometimes very creative, occasionally mavericks. Often they use very expressive, rapid body language. They might say something like, "Can you *picture* this great big balloon, with loads of wacky colours on it, floating away into the distance as if..." at the same time as knocking someone's glass onto the floor.

> Are you a visual person? If not, think of someone you know who is. Do you get on with them or do you wish they'd calm down?

If that's the type of person to whom you talk politely when in fact you're thinking that they're some kind of crackpot, then your mind method is probably not the same as theirs. If it's all too quick and frenzied for you, and your internal voice is saying, "Uhhh, I wish he'd slow down a bit, he's doing my head in," when they launch into, "Can you *see* what I mean? Just *picture* it?" then you may find yourself heading for the door.

If it's just not *clicking* for you, then you may not be a visual person. Your mind method might be the second type. If you're an *auditory* person then you're likely to use phrases such as "I *hear* what you say," or "that *rings a bell*". Auditory people tend to speak at a more normal speed with less fluctuation in pitch; their voices tend to be more measured and rhythmic. Words mean a lot to them and they are often very careful about what they say. They tend to be more ordered and structured in their lives and use expressions like "That *sounds* good to me."

> Are you an auditory person? If not, think of someone who is. Do you get on with them or do they irritate the hell out of you?

They may be talking to another person though, who is struggling with their communication style. "What do you have to *say* about it?" they ask, but the other person doesn't have much to say about it at all. They may just want to shrug their shoulders and pull a face, or take a deep breath. This is the *kinaesthetic* person, who, by and large, does not always like to communicate with spoken language. He or she likes to develop a *feel* for what you are saying, a *gut feeling*. They might say, "I think I'm *in touch* with what you're putting across."

Kinaesthetic people often talk very slowly, sometimes with a lot of deep breaths between sentences, or even words. Their voices tend to be deep and they often use a lot of metaphors from the physical world. Kinaesthetics want to "grasp" what you're saying. Everything that happens to them in their lives is interpreted by their feelings. They do tend to get on extremely well with other kinaesthetic people, but sometimes bore the life out of auditory people, and especially visual people, who are already racing on to the fifth new concept as the kinaesthetic person finishes each sentence.

> Imagine two people meeting each other for the first time, one very laid back and kinaesthetic, the other ultra-visual Mr/Ms thousand-miles-per-hour. Can you imagine them creating an instant rapport? What happens in your mind's eye?

Now imagine two hugely visual people together, waving their arms around in the air, chattering away nineteen to the dozen, each trying to get a word in edgeways to take the conversation onto some further creative astral plane. Yet they are in perfect harmony with one another, laughing, joking and obviously hugely stimulated by each other's company.

> Try the same exercise imagining two auditory people together.

Beware! Before you start putting yourself and other people into neat little boxes labelled "visual", "auditory" or "kinaesthetic", you

need to be aware that nearly everyone operates on a composite of the three different methods, and will use all of them at different times. Having said that, for almost all of us one of the mind methods will be dominant.

Place yourself into your ideal scenario. Imagine that it's you who's in perfect harmony and rapport with someone. What words are they using, how quickly are they speaking, what's their intonation like, how much body language are they using? This should give you a clue as to what type of predominant mind method you have.

There are many non-verbal aspects to good communication:

1. When all else fails, third parties can mediate in disputes.
2. The body mirrors the mind. Analysing someone's body language can give you an insight into their thoughts and feelings.
3. Good communications depend on rapport, and that comes down to a feeling of "This person's just like me."
4. People have visual, auditory or kinaesthetic mind methods. Use the same approach to communicate with them most effectively.
5. To communicate effectively and completely practise matching and mirroring and understanding everything about other prople, from body posture and breathing pattern to the speed and tone of their voice.

PEOPLE ARE DIFFERENT

Chapter 3

What's in this chapter for you

> *Distinguishing between matchers and mismatchers*
> *Rules for confident communication*
> *Dealing with difficult people*

Matching and mismatching

If you look, it's easy to see that people are different. It's not just different mind methods that make people respond differently, there's another area of people's communication style that is useful to know and learn about in the future.

> Place three coins, of different value, on a table, and ask a friend to describe what they see. Note their description. Is it the same as yours? Try it with several different people.
>   People respond differently to this exercise. One person may say "It's all money," or "They're all coins," or "They're all round." This person is a **matcher**.
>   Another person may answer totally differently. He or she may say "They're all different," or "There are different coins, with different values." This person is a **mismatcher**.

Matchers look for similarities between things; mismatchers look for differences. They are both equally valid ways of processing information, but if you know which method someone prefers, you'll find it much easier to get them to respond to you.

> Think about some of the people you work with or see regularly. Are they matchers or mismatchers? Try them out with the coin test and see if you're right. How could you deduce which they are without doing the test?

In neuro-linguistic programming this way of sorting things, by similarity or difference, is called a *metaprogram*. I prefer to call them motivation methods; it's easier to remember, for one thing!

There are lots of them, and they are worth learning about because they are a real key to understanding how other people operate. Understanding motivation methods might help you clinch a business deal, or find a partner for life!

Here are some of the more important differences between the ways that people sort and process information:

- *similar/different*
- *attention to self/attention to others*
- *internal motivation/external motivation*
- *approval of self/approval of others*
- *small (details)/big (picture)*
- *"I should"/"I could"*
- *moving away from painful outcomes/moving towards pleasurable outcomes*
- *proactive/reactive.*

Some people are motivated by what they can have or can achieve, whereas others are driven by what they can't have or can't achieve. Some people are motivated to seek pleasurable outcomes, and others are motivated to avoid the displeasure or pain of certain outcomes. Some people are motivated by their own judgement and approval, while others depend upon the appraisal or recommendation of others. In this instance you may find you need the approval of someone's friends, business colleagues or boss, before you can really communicate well with them.

Here's an example. My young son went through a long period of being a mismatcher. When I picked him up from school I would ask him what he'd done at school that day. "Nothing much really," he'd respond. However hard I tried I used to draw a blank. Then I discovered the power of understanding motivation methods. One day I picked him up from school and said to him, in a fairly gruff voice (matching his style of the moment), "I bet you've done nothing much really at school today have you?" I had to stop the car to listen as he reeled off every event of the day, almost in protest. So understanding and matching someone's motivation method can be like having the key to a locked door.

Can you think of an example in your life, like the one above, where someone just does not communicate with you? When this happens try matching their style and see what happens.

With practice you can become adept at working out how other people like to process information just by talking to them, and you can use this knowledge to improve your communications with almost anybody. Occasionally, however, you might meet a very strong mismatcher who tends to disagree with nearly everything you say. You may find it difficult to develop a close relationship here because they simply don't think in the same way as you. Mismatchers tend to be fault-finders, so they're the ideal people to have checking aeroplanes for take-off and a thousand other jobs where sorting by difference is invaluable. It's in their nature, but it can make them difficult to live with!

The list above is far from exhaustive. There are many more motivation methods that people use; indeed, whole books have been written just on this subject. It's an advanced communication skill, but worth learning if you want to become a master communicator.

> Next time you would like a mismatcher to do something, simply suggest that they do the opposite to what you want and watch what happens.

However, the fact remains that no matter how much knowledge you acquire you'll not be able to put it into practice and become a good communicator if you lack a certain level of confidence.

Twenty "rules" for confident communication

What makes one person more confident than the next? The answer is experience and practice. If your early communication experiences as a child weren't fruitful then it's entirely possible that you experienced a kind of communication shutdown; one where you tended to talk only when you had to.

To gain confidence in your communicating it's important to understand that you're not the only one who lacks a little confidence or possibly has a slightly less than average self-opinion or self-worth.

> How confident are you when you speak to other people? Does your level of confidence go down in front of people in authority, or large groups of people? How about public speaking; addressing an audience?

Over many years of studying core and applied psychology I've formulated my own opinions about the way people in general perceive the world. I discovered that we all share much in common. I developed a set of twenty "rules" that I felt would help people to understand and deal with others. To an extent they're a bit of fun, yet I believe that there is a very serious side to them. They reflect one of my core beliefs – that most people are nothing more than children in adult bodies, with some added life experience.

My personal belief in these rules has helped me to be able to deal with absolutely anyone with confidence: whether it's the chairman of a large corporation or a hooligan with threatening behaviour I don't feel intimidated. I actually believe that if you adopt the same outlook on people as these rules suggest, then you will gradually achieve added insight into people as well as gaining self-confidence in all of your communications.

> As you read through the "rules", take time to reflect on each one and decide whether it matches your personal experience.

Rule number one: Everyone is still a child, regardless of age, and everyone still needs the basic acceptance, attention and emotional stroking that children need.

Rule number two: Ninety-nine per cent of the population have less than adequate self-worth, self-esteem, self-confidence, and self-image.

Rule number three: The other one per cent are lying.

Rule number four: People don't care how much you know. They do, however, know how much you care! Learn to express, not impress!

Rule number five: Big listeners are popular. Big talkers are often lonely.

Rule number six: A compliment is worth a thousand presents.

Rule number seven: Everyone must be forgiven, unequivocally and permanently. Whatever they may have done they're nothing but products of their own childhood. Anger and bitterness eat away at and destroy those who harbour the feelings and not those towards whom they are directed.

Rule number eight: People who are angry are often those who are hurting most themselves.

Rule number nine: Everyone would like to have more control over at least one aspect of life, and everyone needs at least one person to whom they can open up completely.

Rule number ten: No one really cares if you make a fool of yourself. Everyone is far too busy thinking about themselves and their own problems to care much about yours.

> If some of the "rules" challenge your current ways of thinking, try asking yourself, "What would happen if I adopted that rule, and what would happen if I acted as though it were true?"

Rule number eleven: There's no such thing as rejection, simply a refusal of the product currently on offer. Don't take it personally!

Rule number twelve: Everybody communicates differently: with words, feelings, pictures or gesticulations. To create rapport with them you need to communicate in the same way they do.

Rule number thirteen: People that are like each other, tend to like each other. Opposites do attract, but often they eventually repel and destroy each other.

Rule number fourteen: Do suffer fools gladly. There is actually no such thing as a fool, simply someone less fortunate or less gifted than you, and you can learn from everyone.

Rule number fifteen: Never try to change someone (especially children). It becomes a statement that you do not like them.

Rule number sixteen: People often do not mean what they say, yet they don't often say what they mean!

Rule number seventeen: He who wins the argument loses the war.

Rule number eighteen: If you spend too much time thinking about yourself, then you're likely to end up by yourself.

Rule number nineteen: Don't let anybody bounce cheques in your emotional bank account. Nobody, but nobody, has the right to chop you down and make you feel small, without your permission.

Rule number twenty: The Immutable Law of Life can be stated in many ways. Here are three versions:

> *What goes around has a habit of coming around, although you might not receive back directly from the hand to whom you gave.*
> **– Unknown**

> *As you sow, then so shall you reap.*
> **– The Bible**

> *If you are not getting what you want back out of people, and life, then you are simply not putting enough in.*
> **– Webster's Law of Reciprocity**

> Now you have read the twenty "rules", choose one or two that really made you think and put them into action. Live with them and by them for a week and see what happens.

Understanding loudmouths

I would like to take one of the rules and put some flesh on it. It's rule number four: People don't care how much you know. They do, however, know how much you care! Learn to express, not impress! Being an over-the-top, brash, flash, all-talking, non-listening, pretentious, "mine's bigger and better than yours" type of loud-mouthed social bully isn't big and it's not clever!

The animal referred to in rule number four is normally male. Every time you meet him he has a new story to tell you about something he has done better than you and everyone else. He could have always played that particular sport much better (when he was still playing, that is!), he knows how to do your job better than you, how to run the National Health Service; indeed, how to run the country.

> Do you know anyone like this? How do you normally react when they buttonhole you?

In fact, his knowledge of all subjects is greater than yours and he loves to remind you of it with great regularity. The acceleration and the top speed of his car are better than yours. His new watch just cost him a fortune, but he's already told you that he earns enough to afford things like that easily. His house is bigger than yours, or he's just bought a second house abroad, his garden is bigger, his wife (to whom he is usually downright rude) is more attractive, his children are naturally gifted and his dog – a rare pedigree, of course – won at Crufts. His conversations always start with "I" or "When I was" or "When I used to . . .". He also interrupts you in mid-flow, usually starting with "I" again, and regularly barges into conversations.

These people are not easy to like. But they are much easier to understand when you realise that they have the weakest ego or self-esteem of all.

Why does it happen? Well, self-esteem is often unwittingly damaged in the home environment when children are very young, and the first opportunity that most children have to try and repair their self-esteem is with other children, at play and at school. The silent types endure alone, never assert their presence in their peer group and often suffer a further lowering of self-esteem by default. More outgoing children, however, play the game of "mine's bigger and better than yours". This is the best method that many young children have of asserting some authority and control over their fellows. It becomes the best weapon in their arsenal to bolster their own self-esteem.

> **Watch any group of small children playing together and you'll observe them playing the "mine's bigger and better than yours" game.**

Our loud-mouthed friend could have started out either way. Perhaps he never grew out of the habit of increasing his own self-esteem at the expense of others, and failed to adapt to the adult world. Or possibly, having suffered in silence for many a long year, he finally enters that big wide adult world, losing contact with his former peers and seeking an audience with all and sundry to practise on them what has been practised upon him for so long. Now he attempts to hold court with anyone within spitting distance, but pays them no real attention. He is, incidentally, about the worst type of boss that you could ever have. The only management "skill" he's ever learned is that of putting others in their place.

> **Start to become an observer of life. Note the ways in which adults as well as children interact and see if you can spot some of the games they play.**

PEOPLE ARE DIFFERENT

The loudmouth is a sorry fellow in many different ways. And the key to understanding how to deal with this chap lies in a funny sort of reversal. It would help you greatly to actually feel sorry for him. Remember that he's an emotionally undernourished child in his own right. If you help him to like himself by stroking his ego you'll be doing him a great favour and you'll have opened up a channel of communication which you can use to put your point across.

Remember rule number one: Everyone is still a child, regardless of age, and everyone still needs the basic acceptance, attention and emotional stroking that children need. If you can feed that need then it will assist you with all of your communication with people. It will also help them to like you. Emotional food is actually in quite short supply, in case you hadn't noticed, and it therefore commands a very high value in the marketplace.

Many people think of communication as talking. Yet the ability to listen carefully and attentively is a quality that will stand you in greater stead than the ability to talk the hind legs off a herd of donkeys.

It's important to realise that people are different:

1. Learn to recognise and deal with matchers and mismatchers.
2. People act from different motivators so discover what they are and feed them.
3. Variety is the spice of life! Value diversity, seek other people's opinions, learn from them and add to your store of knowledge.
4. Be flexible. If you're naturally a matcher, look for mismatches; if you tend to focus on details, try looking at the big picture for a change. The more flexible your approach the more doors you open in life.
5. Apply the twenty "rules" above. Even if you don't believe in all of them, try putting them into practice and see what happens.
6. Remember the loudmouth. People are not always easy to like, but the more you try to understand them the better your communication with them will be.

FROGS AND AARDVARCS — Chapter 4

What's in this chapter for you

Learning to accept people
Understanding people's needs
Asking open questions
How to listen effectively
Using other people's interests to your advantage

Why asking questions makes you popular

Nearly everyone likes to talk. Indeed one of the golden rules of the therapy profession, which is all about talking and listening, is that everyone needs at least one person with whom they can be totally open and honest. Someone with whom they can openly and unashamedly discuss every little detail of their life, whether it is something from the past, something happening now, or their desires or fears for the future.

> *As long as we are still the only people in the world who listen attentively to people and all of their problems, and accept them, warts and all, then our profession is safe!*
> **– Caroline Westing, psychologist**

This quote tells us something about people. Apart from the core human needs of survival (food, shelter and warmth), there are other psychological needs that you and I have. Abraham Maslow famously postulated a "hierarchy of needs", suggesting that once an individual's basic physiological needs had been met – starting with warmth, food and sexual fulfilment and moving on to a safe, structured environment – then the higher needs of love, esteem and personal fulfilment could be released. These higher needs include: the need to be accepted unconditionally, the need to be appreciated, the need to be respected and recognised, the need to be desired, the need to be valued or to feel valuable, the need to be approved of, and the need to be complimented.

> How do these needs affect the way we communicate with each other? Can you think of examples featuring people you know in which communication fulfils one or more of these needs?

If you break down the art of conversation into two distinct halves then you're either listening or talking. When meeting a new person for the first time most people tend to get the balance wrong. Most of us simply talk too much, and when we do stop talking and start to listen we don't listen very carefully.

Is that really good communication? Does it help to fulfil the other person's needs? Does it make them feel appreciated, recognised, respected or valued? Or is there a better way?

It stands to reason that if two people get together and both are so determined to listen that neither of them speaks, not much conversation will result. So if all talk is not the answer and all listening will not work either, what should we do?

> If you're meeting someone for the first time, then ask lots of questions. Listen carefully to show that you're genuinely interested. Find out about them. As you do this you'll also learn about their mind method and motivation methods. In fact you'll be amazed at the spin-offs from becoming a good question asker and a good listener.

Ask questions: in particular ask what are called "open" questions – ones that cannot be answered with a straight "yes" or "no". You need to exercise some caution – don't be intrusive or impertinent – and be very attentive: if someone steers away from a topic of conversation then don't pursue it, however innocent it might seem. A simple question like "Do you have children?" could be devastating to someone who wants children and can't have them, or who's recently lost a child. But most people will politely steer a conversation away from subjects they don't want to talk about, so just start again on a different topic.

> Practise starting conversations by asking open questions and listening carefully to the answers. See how much you can find out about the other person: their likes and dislikes, their background and personality.

You may feel that you need some help in asking the right sorts of questions. Here's a useful acronym to get you started. When you begin to talk to someone think of FROGS:

- F stands for family and friends
- R stands for recreation
- O stands for occupation
- G stands for geography
- S stands for social life.

You might ask about their *family* – where they are, what they do, are they close? What do they like to do for *recreation*? What do they do after work or during the weekend? What are their hobbies? Ask about their *occupation*. Have they always done that, and what would they like to do? It is remarkable how chatty most people become when the subject of conversation is what they would like to do! The "G" is about *geography*: where do they live, where have they been, and where would they like to go? What do they like to do on holiday? And lastly, their *social life*: when do they like to socialise, who with, and where do they like to go?

> Next time you are in conversation with someone you don't know, think of FROGS. See if you can ask some questions relating to each area. If you struggle, or things seem awkward, try another FROGS topic. Remember, you want them to do the talking.

If you're in sales, you're probably familiar with the idea of asking open questions to uncover someone's needs – and if you're not familiar with it then you need to be! But think about this for a moment: aren't we all in sales? If you go for a new job, or ask someone out on a date, you are selling. You're selling yourself, a proposition or an idea in most of the things you do. And if you're

forty-three

married then you certainly sold someone on that idea! At the heart of all these transactions lies good communications, and the core skills of questioning and listening.

Improve your listening skills

Of course, to maintain this sort of conversation you do have to listen well, and you have to cultivate the art of remembering what has been said to you. And that is perhaps not as easy as it sounds. Many people have difficulty in listening carefully and taking in what is being said to them. So here's a tip: try to engage all of your senses whilst listening. Most people simply listen to the words that are being said to them, but the human brain stores pictures, feelings, smells and tastes more effectively than words.

> **Think back to a conversation you had a while ago where someone was explaining to you something that was important to them. See how many of their actual words you can recall. Now think in pictures about what they were telling you. Add in sounds, colours, feelings, tastes and smells. How vivid is the memory now?**

When you're listening to someone, make what they're telling you into a movie. Add pictures in your mind to the words that are being said. Make the pictures move, and make them as big, as bright and as colourful as you can. If it's appropriate then make the pictures bizarre or unusual: the brain remembers things that are out of the ordinary. You can try distorting the images or making them funny. Do remember though that you're doing this to aid your memory. Don't get so carried away that you're not listening to the other person at all, or that you start laughing at your own images! Once you become adept at the process, start adding in sounds and linking feelings to your movies. Put the tastes and smells in too, and exaggerate everything.

If you do this well you'll start to enjoy the process of listening more. Indeed, rather than simply waiting your turn to speak – the worst non-listening habit of all – you may find that you actually prefer listening to talking! This will make you more popular, and at the same time improve your recall of what has been said.

> Try this new memory aid as soon as you can. Associating bizarre or unusual images with things is a well-known technique used by memory specialists. Like all such techniques it needs practice if you're to be good at it, but it is a learned skill. The more you do it the better you'll become at recalling everything that's said to you.

Of course, you cannot simply ask questions all the time; a conversation is not an interrogation and you need to add to it in an interesting way. The easiest times at which to do that are when you find points of common interest, but avoid one-upmanship: remember, it's not big and it's not clever. It also makes the other person feel either less about themselves and their achievements, or it makes them think that you're a big-head. As you do listen and respond, remember those needs we talked about.

If you ask good questions, listen well and provide emotional food in your conversations, you'll gradually gain a respect and self-confidence that will reap huge dividends for you. Some of those basic human needs mentioned earlier, and that you too need, will start to be repaid to you. By and large people appreciate, respect and value others who are great listeners! Remember the principle behind rule number twenty: you get back what you put into life.

Why people need AARDVARCs

Acronyms are a great way of remembering things. So let's look at those human needs in more detail and use an acronym to remind you of them. The word AARDVARC (spelled with a "C" at the end) might help here. Let's take a further look at the AARDVARC method of feeding people's emotional needs.

The first word is *appreciation*. Take the scenario of meeting someone for the first time in a business situation. You tell him or her that you appreciate them taking the time out of their busy schedule to see you. For the purpose of this exercise let's use a male example.

By telling him that you really appreciate him taking the time to see you, you just stroked his ego and he likes that. He likes himself a little more thanks to you and he starts to like you straightaway. He doesn't like those who don't appreciate him, his position within the company, and how valuable his time is. He feels that if they don't appreciate him then they possibly have the opposite attitude to appreciation: depreciation.

You notice his reaction and make a mental note to remind him again at the end of the meeting that you appreciated his time. If you're really clever you'll find several topics during your meeting whereby you can elicit his thoughts or his wisdom on a particular subject and tell him how much you appreciate his knowledge on that particular subject. You might also remember the Law of Psychological Reciprocity if you get to a sticky point in the meeting. It works like this: if you tell him that you appreciate his view, his feelings, or what he is saying he will almost certainly express appreciation of, and give you credit for, the next thing that you say. Try it – it works.

> Make a mental note to try out the Law of Psychological Reciprocity and see what results you get.

The next word is *acceptance*. Acceptance is the one thing above all others that human beings strive for. It is the one food that we all hunger for more than any other.

> " You will never forcefully change someone else, but by liking that person as he or she is and helping them to like themselves even more, you will give them the most amazing power to change themselves. "
> **– Carl Adams, psychoanalyst**

One of the deepest desires of mankind is to find others with whom we can be completely relaxed. For most of us it's one very special person and we seem prepared to go to any lengths to find that person. The reason we do this is because we all have a deep need to find someone with whom we can simply let our hair down, relax and be accepted for who we are; someone who loves us for what we are, warts 'n' all, and someone with whom we can discuss absolutely anything and everything without fear of rejection or admonishment; someone who's closer than close.

FROGS AND AARDVARCS

> *" Away from the pretence we make to the rest of the world as to who and what we are not, everyone needs at least one person in whom they can confide one hundred per cent. "*
> **– Virginia Swann, psychoanalyst**

To a greater or lesser degree that same basic need is applicable to everyone you come into contact with. The more you accept them for what and who they are, and the more they accept you for what and who you are, the closer you come to them.

> *" The need to be totally accepted for who you are by your partner at home, your parents and anyone else you are particularly close to is of paramount importance. If human beings go home to nagging, scolding, critical, whinging, fault-finding partners or parents it gnaws away at and erodes the very foundation of their character and self-esteem, and eventually turns that person against the other out of self-protection. The result of this sort of behaviour is that the relationship degenerates in a fast-moving downward spiral. The opposite is of course true: loving, supportive relationships can help people achieve things they would not have managed, or perhaps even aspired to, on their own. "*
> **– Timothy Jenkins, psychoanalyst**

How supportive are you of those closest to you? Do you accept them for who and what they are, or do you find fault and seek to change people? Remember: what you get out of life, and that includes relationships, depends upon what you put in.

There is only one "R" next in "AARDVARC", but we can use it to remember both respect and recognition. Let's revisit the meeting with the businessman. You're in the office and the meeting is going well. At the appropriate time you mention that you have a lot of respect for the way he handled a particular project. You just stroked his ego again. He likes being respected and recognised for his ability so he likes himself a bit more. He is starting to really like you now. You definitely notice that and the whole meeting starts to relax a little. Because you can see he likes you, you like

forty-seven

yourself more and your confidence increases. Once more you make a mental note to use the word "respect" again when the moment is right. It's a very effective word, but not one to be used lightly: insincere compliments soon show.

> **The next time you ask someone for advice, tell them how much you respect their opinion.**

The next word is *desire*. It is another ego food that everyone is hungry for. Indeed there is a worldwide famine, yet you have a plentiful supply. It is not quite so easy to introduce into a business meeting, but remember that everyone needs to feel as if they're desirable.

The next word is *value*. People like to feel valuable and valued whether it's in business or any other relationship. During the meeting you could say, "I would value your opinion on this issue". It's like saying, "I know you're an intelligent person," which is a strong ego-stroke. On the way out you could tell the businessman how much you enjoyed the meeting and valued his input on a certain issue.

Our next word is *approval*. As children we all seek approval: from parents and other relations, and approval from peers. A child seeking approval brings a painting home from school to show to a parent, yet often receives little more than a cursory glance or, even worse, a comment like, "I haven't got time right now. Show me later." But the moment has gone and the lack of approval is often mistaken for disapproval. Most children receive enough disapproval as it is and tend to grow up seeking approval at all times.

> **Do you ever turn people away who may be seeking approval from you? We're all busy, but sometimes, especially with children, "later" just won't do.**

The need for approval doesn't go away as people get older. To make approval work for you, take the time to look at things people have created or prepared and show a genuine interest. Even if something isn't quite right you can still begin with approval, using statements like, "I can really see where you're coming from on this; it's good work." Praise first and then suggest modifications. If you're in management this will get much better results than saying, "No, that's all wrong. Take it away and do it again."

The next word is *reassurance*. Everyone needs reassuring at some stage or other. With shock victims the first thing they require after being made physically warm and comfortable is reassurance. Children need continual reassurance. Employees and partners in relationships need reassurance from time to time. Your bank manager needs reassuring sometimes, especially if things are not going too well for you. The stock market seeks reassurance from the banks and other financial institutions. The government seeks reassurance: from the stock market in order to plan and orchestrate its fiscal policies, and from other governments regarding the safety of borders, trade agreements and so on.

Even if you think everything is working out well for you in a particular situation, remember that the other person might not feel so sure. From the tiniest child to the largest organisation in the world, everyone needs reassurance.

> Take some time to think who around you might need reassurance. Someone at home, a work colleague, a customer or client, perhaps even your bank manager! Work out what you need to do or say to provide that reassurance, then do it! Make reassurance a habit.

The final word is *compliment*. In the twenty rules, rule six states that a compliment is worth a thousand presents. It costs absolutely nothing to pay someone a compliment, yet it has a remarkable effect upon the person who's receiving the compliment. When you use compliments try and personalise them – by this I mean complimenting the action rather than the result. Instead of saying "I like your dress," or "I like your car," try saying "I really like your choice of clothing," or "I really like your choice in cars." This is a much more sophisticated way of complimenting. It is also much more personal because it compliments the person as well as the product.

Being interested all the time

> " *If you're a good listener and you make other people feel good about themselves, you'll find yourself making new friends wherever you go. If you do this well when meeting anyone for the first time, even if you haven't said very much at all, they're likely to go away thinking to themselves, 'What an interesting person that was. I'd like to get to know them better.' I couldn't operate without this ability.* "
> – **Jim Trustram, entrepreneur**

So there you are, still stuck in that meeting with the businessman. You look around the room for something that isn't too obvious and something that you're genuinely interested in. When the time is right you say to him that you're very interested in the little toy soldiers on the shelf.

Wow. Does he like that or what? You're interested in something that he's interested in and that nobody's ever noticed before. He's feeling very good right now. All those salespeople that come into the office admire the paperweight on his desk or they mention the stupid plaque on the wall, and he knows they're being false. So, what is the difference when you notice the toy soldiers? The difference is that you're genuinely interested in knowing what makes him tick: his interests are interesting to you.

> How do you feel when someone expresses an interest in your particular hobby, or a subject you feel passionate about? And how do you feel about that other person when this happens? You can share that feeling with others by being interested in their passions.

You both wander over to look at the toy soldiers. You notice that they're hand painted and take a gamble by saying how well they're painted. He volunteers that his thirteen-year-old son painted them, and you're genuinely impressed. You tell him so.

He positively beams with delight. You get into a conversation about his son and his other children. You talk about the things they do together as a family and you tell him that his kids are very lucky to have a dad like him.

You just paid him several compliments and told him how much you approve of and respect his parenting ability. It's important to do this with integrity, though. If you try to use this as some sort of slick technique, spraying compliments around while privately thinking very different thoughts, it won't work for you.

> The key is to be interested from the beginning. Think to yourself: I wonder what this person's mind methods are? I wonder what motivates this person? I wonder what they enjoy doing outside work? People are fascinating if you just take the trouble to find out a little about them. Feed their ego and needs.

Remember the AARDVARC method:

- A = appreciation
- A = acceptance
- R = respect and recognition
- D = desire
- V = value
- A = approval
- R = reassurance
- C = compliment.

Remember also one of the first laws of economics, "supply and demand", and remember that ego food is in hugely short supply yet in universal demand. If you become a supplier of that food then you will also be in great demand.

And remember finally that you must not ask a price for it, especially with children, and that you must supply it with sincerity. Otherwise it has no value whatsoever.

Learn how to get the most from people:

1. Asking open questions makes for good conversations, and good conversationalists are popular.
2. All good conversationalists have good openers. Remember FROGS and you can get into conversation with anyone.
3. Become a great listener by really paying attention. Improve your recall by involving all your senses, not just remembering the words.
4. We all have the same needs. The more you meet other people's needs the more you will get the things you want from life.
5. The AARDVARC feeds people's emotional needs.
6. To be interesting, be interested.

SPECIFICALLY SPEAKING
Chapter 5

What's in this chapter for you

Avoiding miscommunications by using specific language
How to make decisions effectively
Improving your command of English
Answering tricky questions
Boosting your self-confidence

Precision model

> *" I got into a heated argument with a colleague in a meeting once. Our boss quickly stepped in with a simple question addressed to both of us. We quickly realised that neither of us really knew what point the other was trying to make. It was an embarrassing case of communication breakdown. "*
> **— Daniel Dougherty, marketing coordinator**

Have you ever felt that you were caught up in a conversation that was going nowhere? One where the conversation was so fluffy or woolly that in the end it all became meaningless? Have you ever been asked a question that you couldn't answer, only to work out exactly what you wanted to say some time later?

All these situations have one thing in common: they are miscommunications of one sort or another. Miscommunications usually happen because words mean different things to different people. Getting people to be specific about what they're trying to say is an art form that can be learned. It will also make all of your conversations with people much more fruitful.

If you do ever get caught up in silly arguments, and most of us do from time to time, the next time it happens try this: ask the other person to define their terms exactly, and you do the same. One of two things will happen. Either you will find that you actually agree, or, more likely, you will very rapidly end up saying, "Well, we'll just have to agree to differ about that."

Richard Bandler and John Grinder, the founders of neuro-linguistic programming (NLP), started out trying to model excellent communicators in the field of psychotherapy. In doing so they found that they had to use language itself to clarify language – they had to find ways of using words that would enable them to be very specific about what people were saying. This is called the *meta-model* in NLP-speak, but *precision model* is a more descriptive name.

If someone says to you, "Kids have it easy nowadays," what do they really mean? Do they mean their kids? Someone else's kids? All kids? That surely can't be true, can it? Starving African kids can't be having "it" easy, can they? And what is this "it" anyway? Funny how vague that remark is once you start to look at it. In order to cut through this kind of muddled talk the precision model suggests simple clarifying questions. So when someone says, "Kids have it easy nowadays," you could ask, "All kids?"

If someone were to say, "People just don't understand me," then a useful question might be, "What specifically is it that people don't understand about you?"

> You can try this on yourself too. Do you ever say, "I should do this"? Or perhaps you more often say, "I shouldn't do that"? Next time you find yourself saying or thinking those words ask yourself, "What exactly is it that stops me from doing it? And, come to that, what would happen if I did do it?"

A lot of salespeople know one or two questions from the precision model. One very good one is in reply to the complaint, "It costs too much!" If you respond by asking, "Compared to what?" you may uncover a wholly unfounded set of assumptions about the price. The worst that can happen is that you're given an exact comparison with some other product in the marketplace, and then you know where you stand with the customer. That's because with this model you're communicating precisely.

That's the gist of the precision model. It's designed to get people to snap out of woolly talk and generalisations into specifics. One word of warning, however: a lot depends upon how you ask these questions. Remember all that stuff about body

SPECIFICALLY SPEAKING

language and tonality? If you just snap these questions out at people and stand there with a big grin on your face looking like a smart alec you may get a much more precise answer than you bargained for – and it may not be in words! Have a care for other people's sensibilities.

> Here's another interesting and useful question to have in your store of responses. If someone replies to one of your questions with, "I don't know," try asking this question very quickly: "What would you say if you did know?". It nearly always elicits an answer:
> "How many sticks are there in the box?"
> "Oh, I don't know!"
> "Well, if you did know what would you say?"
> "Urrf. Oh, two hundred and fifty."
> Try it!

A long time before Bandler and Grinder invented the precision model, the foundations were laid for it with a few lines that have been taught to journalists down through the ages:

> **"** *I keep six honest serving men*
> *They taught me all I knew*
> *Their names are What and Why and When*
> *and How and Where and Who.* **"**
> **– Rudyard Kipling**

Most questions in the precision model start with one of those "six honest serving men" and add the word "exactly" or "specifically", though there are many other ways of eliciting precise meaning and cutting through woolly talking and thinking, but if you remember to ask simple questions like these you will achieve two things. Firstly, you will create more interesting conversations and find out much more specific information. Secondly, you will win friends. Misunderstandings please no one. Used thoughtfully and carefully, with respect for other people's feelings, the precision model can do a great deal to improve personal relationships.

Five powerful words

There's one other incredibly useful expression, and it's one I teach in sales training. It's directed towards decision making, and people are generally afraid of making decisions. Some studies have claimed that we suffer temporary insanity prior to making decisions, and certainly some decisions can be extremely stressful. Stress comes largely from uncertainty; a decision as simple as whether to call "heads" or "tails" involves uncertainty about what will happen. Sometimes that uncertainty is compounded because people have not considered the consequences of the decision, for example whether they can afford something or whether some other person might be unhappy about the decision. If you're selling, there's a whole host of possible consequences that may be on the mind of your customer: the consequences of the effectiveness of your service or the product's reliability, shape, size, suitability, weight, packaging, colour, quality, longevity, for example.

> It stands to reason that if you knew you'd feel totally happy with the consequences of a decision that you have to make, then you'd make that decision right now. So if you're in a selling situation, and your customer doesn't want to order straight away, is it not highly likely that you haven't satisfied his or her qualms about the consequences of the decision?

The magic words to use at this point are, "*What would have to happen...?*" "*What would have to happen* for you to do business with us?" "*What would have to happen* for you to buy this right now?" And these five powerful words are just as useful in other areas.

Suppose a friend says to you, "I would really love to spend more time with my family," and you were to reply, "What would have to happen for you to be able to do that?" Might they start to think about *how* they could do that instead of just vaguely wishing it could happen? It's an empowering question.

> Remember and practise using the five magic words: "What would have to happen...?" And don't forget that these questions are not just for you to ask other people. Before you start practising on others, practise on yourself. Think of an area of life where you'd like to move forward but aren't making the progress you'd like, and ask yourself, "What would have to happen...?"

When you use these five very powerful words people actually change their state of mind. They start to place themselves in the position of having already bought your product or service, or of being in the situation they would like to be in. It's like opening up a blocked channel and showing the way forward.

You can use these five words in lots of different circumstances. If a friend tells you that they're feeling a little low, ask, "What would have to happen for you to feel happier?" Nine times out of ten they'll then plot their own way back into a more resourceful state of mind, or at least know how to solve the problem.

Word power

> *The interviewer asked me whether I'd had any problems using the Metro system. When I told her that maths had always been one of my strong points, she looked at me strangely and her body seemed to shake uncontrollably. I'm glad I didn't get the job: I wouldn't want to work for that sort of nutter.*
> **– Craig Fallon, unemployed security guard**

There's little or no doubt that your command of the English language will have an effect on many aspects of your life. On the one hand it can be embarrassing not to understand the meaning of a word in conversation; on the other it could mean that you don't really understand the whole sentence, which could be particularly awkward if it's a question. That is also very damaging to your self-confidence. For all that we've said about the impact of body language, intonation, and other forms of non-verbal communication, as a general rule most great communicators have a good command of their native language.

That doesn't mean you have to sound as though you've

swallowed a dictionary; in fact quite the reverse. Scholars of language often cite Churchill as an example of great clarity in speech, and he always used the plainest, shortest words he could to express what he wanted to say. English has two roots: Anglo-Saxon and Latin. Churchill favoured Anglo-Saxon, but the Latin root is useful too. Without it the quality known to physicists as the impenetrability of matter would have to be called the ungothroughsomeness of stuff!

> It's no longer necessary to be eloquent, well-spoken, or to have the "right" sort of accent to get on in business or in life (although it does still help in some areas), but a reasonable command of English is important. Take a course if you need to: some evening classes, or whatever suits your purpose best. Learning to make presentations and speak in public, whilst initially very daunting for most people, will reap huge rewards, and is something which anyone can learn to do.

Having the right answers to difficult questions

Whatever you do, never use a word if you're not sure what it means, and if you don't know what someone means when they use a word, then use the precision model. This is also the way to deal with difficult questions. By "difficult" I don't just mean a question which you can't answer. There's an old story that Groucho Marx once listened to a talk on a very technical subject given by an eminent scientist. At the end of the talk the great man beamed at his audience and asked whether anyone had any questions. Groucho had one: "What's the capital of North Dakota?"

> If you don't know the answer then you don't know the answer – and the only thing to do is say so. This leaves us with truly difficult questions, usually ones we *don't properly understand*. You can use the precision model here: you need to clarify exactly what you're being asked, and once you get to that you'll nearly always find that either you do have an answer, or you definitely don't, and can say so clearly.

SPECIFICALLY SPEAKING

Self-confidence – talk it like you walk it

Self-confidence is a vital ingredient in good communication. So what would have to happen for you to be a really confident communicator? For most of us, one of the things that would have to happen has to do with overcoming fear.

> The more you're exposed to something, the less you fear it. So one way to overcome fear is to practise. You do the thing, you get a result, you increase in confidence, you do it again, get a better result, your confidence increases. That's exactly how you learned to walk: every time you fell over, even if you hurt yourself and cried, sooner or later you were back on your feet trying again. You just didn't give up, did you? And you learned how to do it.

Whatever you fear most, then do it. And then, ask yourself what fear means: perhaps "False Evidence Appearing Real" is a bit glib, but it's not far from the truth – it means that you're afraid of the consequences. Nobody's afraid of swimming, but they are afraid of drowning. Nobody's afraid of communicating, but they are afraid of not being liked, not being listened to, not being respected, not being appreciated. Remember the AARDVARC from the previous chapter.

If, however, you start your new era of communication by asking good questions and being a good listener I guarantee that you will start to get pleasant results. Make a point of going out and doing this for the next week or so. As you begin to get pleasant results you will gain a certain confidence. As time progresses your confidence will grow, and as your confidence grows your results will improve further.

> Start asking good questions and being a good listener. Begin with people you feel most at home with, and as your confidence increases try it with people who can make you feel uncomfortable in conversation. Take it one step at a time, but keep practising – it's how you learned to walk, remember!

That's one way to acquire more confidence, another way is quite literally to pretend. Try this now. Assume the complete body posture of someone who appears totally confident. How are they standing? How are they breathing? What type of facial expression are they wearing? How would you act if you were totally confident? If you do this well then your brain chemistry will react accordingly and you will actually feel confident.

> Try to feel confident with your head hung low and a sloppy body posture. Drooping your head, slumping your shoulders and letting your arms hang limply by your sides will almost certainly make you feel depressed, so stop doing it! Our body posture directly affects our state of mind. How often do you put yourself in a poor mental state by adopting a "depressed" posture, or a "tired" posture or a "can't be bothered" posture?

If you learn this art of "pretending" then after a while it will no longer be a pretence. You will learn to be able to put yourself into a confident state of mind by simply changing your body posture and your thoughts. It really does work. In clinical trials in the USA involving patients suffering from long-term depression it was reported that standing up, looking at the ceiling and smiling, even if the smile was completely forced, brought a temporary feeling of well-being.

> You do not have to be depressed to get the feeling of well-being. Try it now. Stand up, look at the ceiling and smile broadly. How do you feel?

Here's another fantastic method for feeling more confident, or powerful, or loving, or anything else you would like: you can give yourself a personality prop, an anchor. The scientist Ivan Pavlov discovered that if he tapped the fish tank every time he fed the fish they eventually recognised the tapping and would rise to the surface even if he did not feed them. He rang a bell every time he fed the dogs and eventually the dogs would salivate at the sound of the bell alone. Has anyone ever used a certain expression that

SPECIFICALLY SPEAKING

sent prickles up your spine instantly? Have you ever heard a piece of music that instantly changed your state of mind? These are all anchors — embedded signals that change your thinking — and you can create your own.

Here's how you do it. Think of a time when you felt very confident about something. It can be anything at all, so take your time if you need to and find a really strong example. Spend a moment or two getting right back into that time: think about what you saw, how you felt, what you were doing, what you heard, and what your "inner voice" was saying to you.

> For this to work you need to get right inside the way you were when you had that experience of real confidence. Don't skimp on this stage — really go for it.

Now, while you are right back inside that experience of confidence, look at your right hand and think of a shape that you could clench in your fist. Give the shape a colour. Stay right in the confident experience, notice the feelings of confidence right through your body, then look at the shape in your hand and clench your fist around it. Then let go. Now do the whole thing again. Then repeat the process, build up the intensity of the confidence, and at the height of the feelings clench your fist again around your shape. Do the whole thing three or four times.

> Now assume the body posture of someone who's extremely confident at communicating with others and imagine yourself growing to twenty feet tall, becoming more and more confident about yourself as you do. And when, and only when, you feel totally confident about your ability to communicate, squeeze your anchor again.

Every time in the future when you feel confident about something, anything at all, then, at the height of the feeling squeeze your shape in your fist. This reinforces the anchor.

That is how you create an anchor, and you can anchor any feeling you have experienced. But how do you use it? Well, once

sixty-one

you've created an anchor you can summon up the feeling by reproducing the anchor.

So if at some stage you feel in need of a little confidence boost, change your body posture to that of being sublimely confident and fire off your anchor by clenching the imaginary coloured shape in your fist. If you have done the process correctly then you'll feel a surge of confidence throughout your body.

There are other aspects to becoming more confident in general.

> **ACT!** If you want to create lots of anchors for different feelings or states of mind it helps to separate them. The "coloured shape" technique works particularly well for most people, but you can squeeze a knuckle between finger and thumb, or squeeze an earlobe, or any similar action. Just make it one you can do unobtrusively in public so that you can use it whenever you want without getting strange looks off people! Think of another state you would like to be able to call up at will and go through the process of anchoring it using a different anchor point.

These things will help you with all of your dealings with, and your influence upon, people. They are: your general attitude toward yourself and others, your beliefs about others and about yourself, your knowledge, your sense of humour, your demeanour and the way you present yourself. The fundamental starting point here is your attitude towards yourself: liking yourself. If you do not like yourself then do not expect anyone else to like you.

The good news is that there is a whole host of books and tapes available to assist you in this area. Invest in the *You Corporation*, because if you don't then nor will anyone else.

People hear your music, not your words

Whether you're reading this book from cover to cover or just dipping in, I hope that you've found some food for thought, and a lot of practical ideas that you can take away and use. Remember that becoming a good communicator is achievable, but, just like learning to ride a bike, it does take time, practice and perseverance.

SPECIFICALLY SPEAKING

> Remember that everyone communicates in slightly different ways and that to communicate effectively with them you must communicate like them.

Remember the twenty rules. They should help you in all of your dealings with people.

Remember also that what you say will never have as much impact, or be as important, as how you say it! A dull message delivered by a charismatic person, filled with energy and enthusiasm, will be accepted as brilliant. An excellent message delivered by someone who lacks vitality and is not interested in the topic, will dampen the enthusiasm of even the most receptive audience.

Possibly the most important thought I can leave you with is this: people hear your music, not your words. If you listen attentively and, when you do speak, you do so with genuine conviction and passion, you will leave your mark on that person indelibly.

To sum up:

1. The clearer your language, the clearer your meaning.
2. Use the precision model on yourself and others.
3. Asking "What would have to happen...?" takes the uncertainty out of decision making.
4. Increasing your vocabulary will increase your confidence.
5. Tackle fear by asking yourself, "What's the worst thing that could happen?"
6. If you feel confident, you'll act confident.
7. People hear your music, not your words.

If you follow the tips and adopt the techniques described in this book you will find an immediate improvement in your ability to communicate with others and this will improve the quality of both your business and private life. GO FOR IT!

Russell Webster also runs his own company, Mindworld. As an exceptionally good speaker and narrator he has developed many audio books to listen to in the car and at home. Although the following titles are available in many bookshops and motorway service stations you can also order them directly.

THE ANSWERS ARE ALL ON MINDWORLD AUDIO TAPES AND CDs

Title	ISBN	Catalogue no.	Author
CASSETTES			
The Critical Childhood Years	1-900165-18-X	MWAC111	Dr. C.M. Vincini
How You Became the Way You Are and How to Make an Enormous Difference in the Life of Your Child!			
The Love Game	1-900165-17-1	MWAC112	Russell Webster
How to Find and Attract the Partner of Your Dreams!			
SUSS-	1-900165-16-3	MWAC113	Russell Webster
The 21st Century Way to Sell Your Product, Your Service or YOURSELF!			
Choices	1-900165-26-0	MWAC119	Russell Webster
Eliminate Fears, Phobias and Uncomfortable Memories and Gain a New Self-Confidence!			
Tomorrow Today (Cassette)	1-900165-27-9	MWAC120	Peter Thomson
The Ultimate Inspiration to Achieving Your Dreams Now!			
The A to Z of Mental Fitness	1-900165-21-X	MWAC114	Russell Webster
A Begginer's Guide to Positive Thinking!			
The History and Future of Management. The Art of Tapping into People Power			
	1-900165-22-8	MWAC115	Brett Lancaster
Financial and Emotional Survival. Safeguarding Your Future With Confidence!			
	1-900165-23-6	MWAC116	Brett Lancaster
A.I.D.A.'s Cat	1-900165-24-4	MWAC117	Russell Webster
The Twenty First Century Way to Write Highly Successful Adverts, Brochures, Mailshot Copy and...			
Wholly Communication	1-900165-25-2	MWAC118	Russell Webster
How to Talk With Confidence!			
7 Secrets Double Cassette	1-900165-19-8	MWAC7	Russell Webster
The Guiding Principles of All Success and Happiness			
MIND YOU DON'T FORGET. Names, Dates, Shopping Lists, Songs, Meetings, Telephone Numbers and Anniversaries:			
HOW TO REMEMBER THEM ALL	1-900165-28-7	MWAC121	Antoine Robinson/Russell Webster
SEVEN SECRETS: Music for the Mind. Inspiring Quotations and Music to Feed Your Mind!			
	1-900165-29-5	MWAC122	Mindmaster
FEELGUD FOR A CHANGE. The Art of Enjoying Yourself!			
	1-900165-30-9	MWAC123	Ed Percival
JUST RELAX FOR A CHANGE. How to Slow Down, Unwind and Rejuvenate Yourself!!			
	1-900165-31-7	MWAC124	Ed Percival
CDs			
Choices CD	1-900165-00 7	CILCD001	Russell Webster
Tomorrow Today CD	1-900165-01 5	CILCD002	Peter Thomson
Mind Explorations...FOUR CDs	1-900165-09-0	CILLMD007	Russell Webster/Peter Thomson

7 WAYS TO ORDER MINDWORLD AUDIOS !
1. MOST GOOD BOOK SHOPS and MOTORWAY SERVICE STATIONS
2. ALL LIBRARIES WILL ORDER YOU A COPY IF YOU QUOTE THE TITLE AND ISBN NUMBER
3. PHONE US NOW ON 01377-257191 FOR A LIST OF SHOPS AND MAIL ORDER SUPPLIERS
4. FAX US ON 01377-256294
5. EMAIL US: POST@MINDWORLD.CO.UK
6. VISIT US AND ORDER ON OUR WEBSITE: WWW.MINDWORLD.CO.UK
7. WRITE TO US AT: MINDWORLD LTD, PO BOX 39, DRIFFIELD YO25 9WH